Loonies and Toonies

A Canadian Number Book

Written by Mike Ulmer and Illustrated by Melanie Rose

Sleeping Bear Press™

310 North Main Street, Suite 300
Chelsea, MI 48118
www.sleepingbearpress.com

THOMSON

GALE

© 2006 Thomson Gale, a part of the Thomson Corporation.

Thomson, Star Logo and Sleeping Bear Press are trademarks
and Gale is a registered trademark used herein under license.

Printed and bound in China.

10 9 8 7 6 5 4 3 2 1

Library of Congress Cataloging-in-Publication Data

Ulmer, Michael, 1959-
Loonies and toonies : a Canadian number book / written by Mike
Ulmer ; illustrated by Melanie Rose.
p. cm.
Summary: "Concepts important to all of Canada are introduced using
numbers. Subjects include languages, famous people, geography, currency,
history, and many more"—Provided by publisher.
pbk ISBN: 978-1-58536-357-5   case ISBN: 978-1-58536-239-4
1. Canada—Juvenile literature. 2. Counting—Juvenile literature.
I. Rose, Melanie, ill. II. Title.
F1008.2.U45 2006
971—dc22   2006002185

For Madalyn.
Number 3.

MIKE

🍁

To my ageless friend Catherine,
one of the kindest and bravest people I know.

MELANIE

1 land, one nation
    that we call home.
  One sense of place
      that's all our own.
    One voice made strong;
        one view made clear
      by the millions of people
          who came to live here.

Canada is home to nearly 32 million people and is the second largest country in size after Russia. Canada is bordered by the Atlantic, Pacific, and Arctic Oceans with the United States to the south.

Our First Nations people are Canada's true founders. Aboriginal people lived here for nearly 10,000 years before Europeans arrived. Their influence shines through in the names of our places such as Saskatchewan (Cree for swift flowing river) and Kanata which means settlement or village in the language of the Iroquois and Huron peoples.

Our country has also been shaped by people who came here from other lands such as India, Italy, Korea, England, Pakistan, Greece, Scotland, China, Iraq, the Ukraine, Ireland, and Somalia. It doesn't matter where you came from or when you arrived, we are all Canadian.

one

1

In the seventeenth and eighteenth centuries, England and France waged a bitter rivalry for control and resources of a vast new land, which was to become Canada. Because of the crucial role of both founding nations, Canada has two official languages, English and French.

Most Francophones live in the province of Quebec but there are pockets of French-speaking people all over the country. Twenty-three of every 100 Canadians list French as their mother tongue. That's why in Canada, writing on everything from cereal boxes to hundred dollar bills is in French and English.

Our First Nations people retain 50 languages of their own including Algonquin, Inuktitut, and Athapascan.

two

2

Here's one thing you should understand—
we use 2 languages in this land.
Marc says vite, Hannah says fast.
One girl's finale is another man's last.
But Canada's a word that's so easy to say,
in English or French it's pronounced the same way.

STOP
ARRÊT

Canadians share an 8,891 kilometre-long border with their neighbours in Alaska, Washington, Idaho, Montana, North Dakota, Minnesota, Michigan, New York, Vermont, New Hampshire, and Maine. The International Border Commission maintains a six-metre path in wilderness areas and also maintains smaller monuments that mark the border.

The number three is very important in Canadian geography. There are three Maritime provinces: Nova Scotia, Prince Edward Island, and New Brunswick, and three prairie provinces: Manitoba, Saskatchewan, and Alberta.

There are also three northern territories: the Northwest Territories, the Yukon, and Nunavut.

three
3

Let's cut a border, 3 metres a side.
You take your half and I'll take mine.
A wandering line, through woods and stone
and running water and mud and loam.
A line that's shared by the best of friends
where Canada begins and America ends.

Located two hours southwest of Toronto, the Stratford Theatre is Canada's most famous stage. It is dedicated to the work of William Shakespeare but other plays are also staged there. When the company began in 1953, the actors performed in a huge circus tent that stood on four 60-foot poles. Theatregoers in the first years remember hearing rain on the canvas and the sound of train whistles from a nearby track. The tent was replaced after three years by a permanent building.

Stratford is a place dedicated to the number four. There are four theatres, the Festival Theatre (1,824 seats), the Avon Theatre (1,093 seats), the Tom Patterson Theatre (487 seats) and the Studio Theatre (260 seats). To alert patrons that the show is about to start, four trumpeters play the Festival Fanfare four times before each performance.

Four was the key number of another great Canadian performance. Quebec strongman Louis Cyr's most famous show of strength came in 1891 when, wearing a special harness, he kept four large draft horses in place while they were urged on by their handlers.

four

4

4 great poles were lifted high
to hoist the canvas into the sky.
Two miles of cable, 10 miles of rope
propped up a town's fantastic hope
that soon this tent could be cast aside
and the shining stars would be the ones inside.

By using the principles of catch and release, outdoorspeople can release their magnificent catches for others to enjoy. The British Columbia fishery produces some of the finest salmon in the world. While most consider five the correct number of salmon types, some scientists believe the Steelhead and the Cutthroat should be classified as salmon as well.

Five Islands Provincial Park in Nova Scotia has one of Canada's greatest views. Not only do 90-metre cliffs overlook the world's highest tides, it's a great spot to learn more about dinosaurs and lava flows. Some fossils from the area are over 200 million years old.

If you like dinosaurs, Canada has one of the world's best sites. The Royal Tyrrell Museum in Drumheller, Alberta is Canada's dinosaur headquarters and is visited by nearly 400,000 people every year. The park is even home to a local dinosaur, the Albertasaurus, discovered by explorer and scientist J. B. Tyrrell who made the find while looking for coal. In fact, he would later find, in Alberta, the largest coal deposits in Canada.

five

5

Of Pacific salmon there are **5** kinds
and all are welcome on fishing lines.
Pink and coho are two of the best.
Chinook and chum are two of the rest.
The sockeye might be the best of the bunch
for catch-and-release or a buttery lunch.

9:30 pm
Newfoundland

00 pm
acific

6:00 pm
Mountain

7:00 pm
Central

9:00 pm
Atlantic

8:00 pm
Eastern

Time zones were invented by a Canadian, Sir Sandford Fleming. Using a world map, Fleming, "the father of standard time," created a system of 24 time zones.

Canada has six time zones, from west to east: Pacific, Mountain, Central, Eastern, Atlantic, and Newfoundland. The island of Newfoundland, which sits in the eastern portion of its time zone, uses Newfoundland Standard Time (NST), half an hour later than Atlantic Time. The Atlantic time zone is in use in most of mainland Labrador, with the southern tip of Labrador following NST.

Six is a great Canadian number. Sap will run inside a maple tree for about six weeks. The Matchless Six were members of the Canadian Track and Field team at the 1928 Olympic Games in Amsterdam, Holland. Bobbie Rosenfeld, Jean Thompson, Ethel Smoth, Myrtle Cook, Ethel Catherwood, and Jane Bell would capture two golds, two silvers, and a bronze medal for Canada.

six

6

With **6** time zones across the land
      your time is based on where you stand.
In Newfoundland when it's half past nine
it's seven o'clock in Central time.
    And out along the Pacific shore
        they've shaved the time by two hours more.

Midway through the 1800s, what is now Canada was a group of six colonies. Everyone agreed on the need for a common purpose, a sense of unity, leadership, and rights and privileges for all. But it took the leadership of Conservative Prime Minister John A. MacDonald to make it happen. MacDonald turned to his trusted friend Georges-Etienne Cartier and Liberal leader George Brown to map out a new vision of the country. By luck, the Maritime Provinces were having similar talks in Charlottetown. New Brunswick and Nova Scotia would decide to enter the union and the framework for a new Canada had been struck. Alexander T. Galt would be Canada's first finance minister. Charles Tupper would operate in cabinets for 25 years. Hector Louis-Langevin, the son of a French soldier, helped draft the text of the British North America Act and would work in MacDonald's cabinet for three decades. D'Arcy McGee, a journalist, poet, and politician would be shot by an assassin in Ottawa in 1868 after giving a fervent speech in support of national unity.

MacDonald, meanwhile, would be remembered as Canada's first prime minister.

seven

7

There were **7** fathers of Confederation,
each with a vision of a brand-new nation.
Langevin, Brown, and Galt made three.
They were joined by Tupper and D'Arcy McGee.
That only left Cartier and the great John A.
to envision a union that endures to this day.

8 left shoes and just one right
to carry him to dark from morning light.
The right shoe never need be new
but the left was always wearing through.
For the hero of Canada's cancer fight
needed eight left shoes, and just one right.

In the spring and summer of 1980, a young British Columbia man named Terry Fox ran 5,376 kilometres in support of cancer research in what he called his Marathon of Hope.

Terry, who had lost his right leg to cancer, had a dream of raising a dollar for every Canadian. To do it, he would run a marathon, 42 kilometres, a day. But Terry's cancer reappeared and he had to stop his run near Thunder Bay, Ontario. Though racked with pain, Terry wouldn't stop until he found a spot where no supporter could see him. He didn't want to let anyone down. The nation mourned when Terry died the following summer at the age of 22. He wore through eight left shoes on his run, but only one at the bottom of his artificial leg. The Terry Fox run is now held in more than 50 countries and has generated more than $350 million for cancer research.

There are memorials to Terry in St. John's, where he took the first step in the Marathon of Hope, in Ottawa in the shadow of the parliament buildings, and in Thunder Bay where his campaign ended.

eight
8

John Ware (1845-1905), a former American slave, was one of Alberta's greatest cowboys. Ware worked a famous 1882 cattle drive that brought 3,000 head of cattle from Utah to the Bar U ranch near Calgary. Once in Canada, he decided to stay. He was legendary for his horsemanship and strength.

In 1884 Ware applied for a quarter section of land and moved his family to Millarville, Alberta. According to legend, the first herd of cattle he owned only had nine head. His quadruple 9 brand eventually became one of the best known brands in the West.

Nine justices on the Supreme Court give the final decision on the most pressing legal issues of the day. Members of the court live and meet in Ottawa. Among the duties of the chief justice is to divide the work of the court among the judges. The judges are selected from all over Canada.

The walk around Vancouver's beautiful Stanley Park is nine kilometres.

nine

9

John Ware started with 9 cattle head
and ended up with several hundred instead.
An Alberta cowboy, as tough as nails
he hustled dogies along the trails.
But he never forgot his earliest times
so he made his brand the quadruple nines.

Canada moved from the old imperial system to the metric system of measurement in 1970. The metric system is based on the number 10 combined with a standard measurement: metre, litre, or gram. For example, a kilometre means 1,000 metres. *Hecto* is Latin for 100, while *deca* is 10 in the Greek language. In the metric system the boiling point of water is usually 100 degrees Celsius. The freezing point of water is zero degrees Celsius.

Ten of the Rocky Mountains in Alberta and British Columbia were named after the women who either climbed them or were prominently involved in mountaineering. That includes Mary Schaffer, an American adventurer who was the first non-native woman to explore what is now Banff and Jasper National Parks.

ten
10

You keep your numbers one through nine
I'll take one-zero, every time.
For size and weight and mass and speed
the metric system's what I need.
There's kilos, grams, and millis, too.
There's tonnes of things that 10s can do!

At 11 a.m., on November 11, 1918, the guns stopped firing in Europe, signaling Armistice and the end of World War I. Canada lost 60,000 of her sons and daughters in the fighting.

Every November 11, at precisely 11 a.m., the nation stops for two minutes of silence to honour the more than 100,000 Canadians killed and 200,000 wounded in war. The tradition of wearing poppies dates back to "In Flanders Fields," a poem written by a Canadian surgeon named John McCrae in the darkest days of World War I. The poem, written after he had spent 17 straight days tending to the wounded, described wild poppies growing between the freshly dug graves of Canadian soldiers.

Because of the worldwide popularity of the poem, the poppy was adopted as the flower of remembrance of lives lost during the war, including those from Britain, France, and the United States.

eleven
11

We bow our heads and start to pray
on the 11th month of the 11th day.
At 11 o'clock the bells are rung.
Across the nation, the hymns are sung.
We wear our poppies to never forget
a sad and never-ending debt.

A dozen is the upper limit of the size of a clutch of Canada geese eggs. The usual clutch contains five to seven eggs but the size ranges from two to 12. Each egg takes a little over a day to lay and a month to incubate. It takes the goslings one or two days to separate from their eggs but they can swim immediately. The Canada goose can be found all over North America, but many commute from Canada to and from the American south. The Canada goose, though famous, isn't our national bird. That honour belongs to the loon. Our national symbols include the beaver, in commemoration of Canada's history in the fur trade, the maple leaf, the central element on the flag, and the maple tree.

In 1946 Viola Desmond, a black Halifax beautician and teacher, was kept in jail for 12 hours and fined $20 after refusing to leave a section of a New Glasgow, Nova Scotia, theatre reserved for white people. Her courageous challenge convinced the province to pass legislation outlawing discrimination.

twelve

12

A dozen little Canada geese—
that's 24 feet, all underneath.
You can look at clutches from coast to coast.
You'll find that **12** is bigger than most.
Twelve in a line, on lakes or hills
not one William, but a dozen bills.

Canada has been growing since it was declared the Dominion of Canada in 1867 with only four provinces: Ontario, Quebec, Nova Scotia, and New Brunswick.

They were followed by Manitoba and the Northwest Territories in 1870 and British Columbia in 1871. Two years later came Prince Edward Island. The Yukon came aboard in 1898.

The new century brought more expansion. Saskatchewan and Alberta joined in 1905. The province referred to as Newfoundland joined in 1949. (In 2001 an amendment to the constitution made official the name Newfoundland and Labrador.) Fifty years later came the newest member of the Canadian family, Nunavut.

The Confederation Bridge, finished in 1997 is just a whisker under 13 kilometres and links Prince Edward Island to New Brunswick and the rest of Canada. The bridge took three and one-half years and a billion dollars to build.

thirteen
13

With 10 provinces and three territories
our nation's a book with **13** great stories
of railways and battles and all those who came;
of badlands and sweetgrass and warm summer rain;
of oceans and valleys and islands and coves
all tucked in one country, our great northern home.

JULY 1

JULY 2

JULY 3

JULY 4

JULY 5

JULY 6

JULY 7

JULY 8

JULY 9

JULY 10

JULY 11

JULY 12

JULY 13

JULY 14

OUR SUMMER TRIP

It takes about 14 days to canoe down the South Nahanni River in the Northwest Territories' Nahanni National Park. The 322-kilometre trek includes a natural hot spring, First Canyon, Canada's deepest river, and Virginia Falls, falls that drop further than Niagara Falls.

There are 41 national parks spread across Canada's provinces and territories. They range from the Wood Buffalo National Park in the Northwest Territories, a park larger than Switzerland (and Canada's biggest) to tiny Point Pelee National Park on Canada's southern tip. Famous for its migrating birds and monarch butterfly, Point Pelee is one of Canada's most unique parks.

The best **14**-day trip you could take
starts from a place called Rabbit Kettle Lake.
On the Nahanni River you'll forget all your cares
but remember the caribou, the moose, and the bears.
Canada's north offers the greatest of sights
from fast running rapids to the great northern lights.

fourteen

14

To go over Niagara that particular way
     had not been her smartest idea that day.
          So Annie Taylor swore that she'd never repeat
          her reckless, daredevilish, and watery feat.
But **15** of them tried, each one of them called
    to gamble their lives by shooting the falls.

"No one should ever do that again," said American Annie Taylor after she went over Niagara Falls in a specially made barrel in 1901. Taylor was the first of 15 people, 13 of them men, to go over the falls in a barrel. Five perished in the attempt.

Of the three falls at Niagara Falls, the Horseshoe or Canadian Falls is the most famous and dramatic, thanks to a 52-metre drop. Canada and the United States share the hydroelectricity generated by diverting the falls' water. About 2.2 million litres flow over the Horseshoe Falls a second, making it the largest producer of hydroelectricity in the world. Twenty percent of the world's freshwater is in the Great Lakes and most of it flows over Niagara Falls.

No wonder, then, that 12 million tourists visit every year to see one of the natural wonders of the world and the world's most famous waterfall.

Just for fun tourists can stand behind a painted barrel and have photos taken as the illustration shows.

fifteen
15

Most calèches have a wheel with 16 spokes. A ride in a calèche, the French word for carriage, is one of the best ways to see historic Montréal or Quebec City. Humans have lived on the site of modern day Montréal for 8,000 years. Jacques Cartier led the first European expedition to the site in 1535. There are countless places to visit in Montréal including the Biodome, the King Edward Pier in the old port region, and the magnificent Notre-Dame Basilica. A walk through the city of Quebec is like a journey through time. The only walled city in North America, the old city is crammed with restaurants, artists, buskers, and musicians.

The fate of British North America was decided in Quebec City, where an attack by British general James Wolfe defeated the forces of the French general, Montcalm in 1759. Both men died in the fighting. The site of the battle, the Plains of Abraham, is a beautiful park that overlooks the old city.

sixteen
16

The clatter of hooves on roadways of stone
under a horse that is white, bay, or roan.
16 spokes in the calèche's wheel—
the sound of cobblestone marrying steel.
Ride a calèche and you'll never forget
the sights and the sounds of seeing Quebec.

Highway 17 divides the city of Lloydminster between Saskatchewan and
Alberta. Two-thirds of Lloydminster's
23,000 people live in Alberta. Lloydminster is the only town or city in Canada
that spans two provincial borders. As for
strawberries, Saskatchewan's berries are
usually picked in the late June or early
July and the hamlet of Strawberry Hills in
North Central Saskatchewan was named
after all the delicious berries that grow
wild there.

Englishman Henry Kelsey was nicknamed
Boy Kelsey. At 17, he was the first inland
explorer for the Hudson's Bay Company in
1884. Kelsey was also the first European
to explore what is now the Prairies.

seventeen
17

I have my strawberries, but I need cream 17
so I scoot across Highway
and go from Alberta to Saskatchewan.
I'm back almost before I'm gone.
It sure is easy on the feet
to cross a border by crossing a street.

She was built to fish but born to race
and she never knew a second place.
We see her often on our dime
a headin' for the finish line.
In **18** years, not one defeat—
that's the *Bluenose*'s winning streak.

The *Bluenose* was built as a fishing schooner in Lunenburg, Nova Scotia. Beginning in 1920, Americans and Canadians held a race to win the International Fisherman's Trophy. The American sailors won the first race. The *Bluenose* was built and entered the next year. She won Fisherman's Cup races whenever they were held until the event was halted by World War II. The original *Bluenose* sank in 1946 during use as a freighter in the West Indies, but using the original plans and some of the same craftsmen, a successor, *Bluenose* II, set sail in 1963. It visits ports all over Nova Scotia and the world. The *Bluenose*, which immortalized a longtime nickname for Nova Scotians, has been on the Canadian dime since 1937.

eighteen
18

He wore **19** upon his back
and stopped the country in its tracks.
In '72 he stole the show
by scoring the game's most famous goal.
No hockey fan will ever forget
the day Paul Henderson found the net!

In 1972 Paul Henderson, a winger for the Toronto Maple Leafs, scored three game-winning goals as Team Canada rallied to win three straight games and defeat a team from the Soviet Union in what came to be known as the Summit Series. The series-winning goal came in the eighth and final game, with just 34 seconds to play.

Fourteen players from that Canadian team are in the Hockey Hall of Fame, as well as two members of the Soviet team. Henderson, who played most of his career for the Leafs, would never score a goal as big as the three game-winners he scored in Moscow.

Nineteen has been worn by such all-stars as Colorado Avalanche star Joe Sakic and retired Detroit Red Wing great Steve Yzerman.

nineteen

19

For most Canadians, royal visits consist of receiving and spending $20 bills.

The link to Britain's royal family and Queen Elizabeth II is a holdover from Canada's days as a British colony. The endorsement from the crown is the final step in turning a Canadian bill into law. The Governor-General or a Supreme Court Justice act for the queen.

Lucy Maud Montgomery, author of the Canadian classic *Anne of Green Gables*, wrote more than 20 novels. Like Anne, Lucy was an imaginative girl who found wonder in people and nature. She was 34 years old when *Anne of Green Gables*, which tells the story of a Prince Edward Island orphan girl, was published in 1908. The story of Anne Shirley has been published and translated worldwide and Lucy Maud Montgomery would later write six sequels to meet the demand of fascinated readers.

twenty
20

Since nineteen-hundred and fifty-three
we've had a kind and gracious queen,
whose visits often come to an end
with every **20** that we spend.
And while our nation now stands alone
we still revere the crown and throne.

50 polar bears on a warm summer day
letting an ice floe take them away.
In a Manitoba harbour, they're easily found
just chillin' and sittin' and hangin' around.
Churchill is a most bearable destination
for four-footed tourists on summer vacation.

There are three ways of getting to Churchill, Manitoba. You can fly. You can take the train, or you can do what the polar bears do and come by ice floe.

Located 1,600 kilometres north of Winnipeg, Churchill is the polar bear capital of the world.

The bears float into Churchill Harbour atop ice floes that carry them more than 150 kilometres from their usual territories. About 300 bears make Churchill home through the summer and fall. The polar bears enjoy southern treats like blueberries and shrubs before they freeze up in November. Polar bears usually eat seals and are the largest carnivores on Earth. The adult males can weigh 680 kilograms, nearly as much as a small car.

Fifty goals is the magic number for National Hockey League players. The great Maurice 'Rocket' Richard became the first player to score 50 goals in 1945.

fifty
50

It takes 100 cents to make a dollar. Until 1987 the dollar bill was the only piece of $1 currency in Canada. But most dollar bills wore out after less than a year. A coin, on the other hand, could last 20 years. The original $1 coin was to have carried the image of two voyageurs paddling a canoe teeming with furs, but the dies for the coins were either lost or stolen between Ottawa and the processing factory in Winnipeg. The Royal Canadian Mint turned to another design of a loon, and the "loonie" was born.

A loonie embedded in the ice at the 2002 Olympic Games in Salt Lake City is said to have helped bring good luck to both the Canadian Men's and Women's gold-medal winning hockey teams.

The toonie, a follow-up to the successful loonie, was put into circulation in 1996. Canadians gave these two coins their nicknames. The mint refers to the loonie officially as a $1 coin and the toonie as a $2 coin.

one
hundred
100

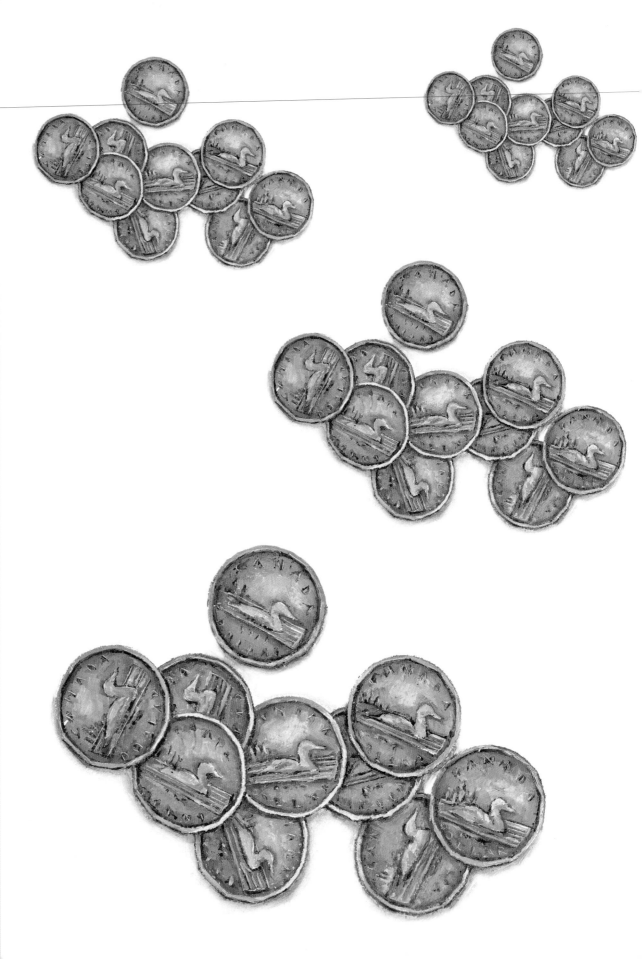

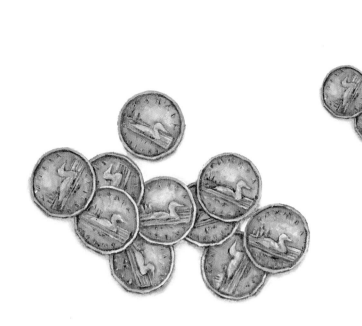

I assume children still had spare teeth
that they hid under pillows, where the fairies could reach.
And the whole magic business was done in the night
and children awoke to find coins in the light.
But where did the fairies get the coins they would trade
before **100**s of loonies and toonies were made?

Mike Ulmer

Mike Ulmer lives in Hamilton, Ontario, Canada, and he has a lot of great numbers. His favorite number is three because he has three daughters, Sadie, Hannah, and Madalyn. The family has four pets, Rudy the dog, cats Sunny and Whiskey, and Sky the horse. He has one wife, Agnes Bongers, which is plenty. Mike has written five books for Sleeping Bear Press, *M is for Maple: A Canadian Alphabet*, *The Gift of the Inuksuk*, *J is for Jump Shot: A Basketball Alphabet*, *H is for Horse: An Equestrian Alphabet* and now *Loonies and Toonies: A Canadian Number Book*. When he isn't writing books for young readers, Mike writes for Maple Leaf Sports and Entertainment, owners of the NHL's Toronto Maple Leafs and the Toronto Raptors of the NBA.

Melanie Rose

Illustrator Melanie Rose's charming and lively oil paintings have graced the pages of several Sleeping Bear Press titles including *Z is for Zamboni: A Hockey Alphabet*; *A is for Axel: An Ice Skating Alphabet*; *H is for Homerun: A Baseball Alphabet*; and the companion alphabet title to *Loonies and Toonies*, *M is for Maple: A Canadian Alphabet*. Melanie is a graduate of the Ontario College of Art. She makes her home in Mississauga, Canada, with her son Liam and their two cats, Mickey and Meesha.